Best wishes,

JIM DAVIS

HELLO AGAIN, GARFIELD FANS!

Welcome to Garfield's second fun-packed
Christmas Annual. We hope you enjoy it even
more than the first. Merry Christmas and a
Happy New Year to all Garfield readers
everywhere.

———

Ravette Books.

THE 1991 Garfield ANNUAL

Created by
JIM DAVIS

Written by
Gordon Volke

Stories by
Jim Kraft

ℛℛ
RAVETTE BOOKS

CONTENTS

Published by Ravette Books Limited 1990

This book is sold subject to the condition that it shall not, by way of trade or otherwise, be lent, resold, hired out or otherwise circulated without the publisher's prior consent in any form of binding or cover other than that in which this is published and without a similar condition including this condition being imposed on the subsequent purchaser.

Printed and bound for Ravette Books Limited, 3 Glenside Estate, Star Road, Partridge Green, Horsham, West Sussex RH13 8RA by BPCC Paulton Books Limited
ISBN 1 85304 276 5

No Telly For Garfield

"Hello, everyone!" said the announcer. "And welcome to another edition of 'Lifestyles of the Fat and Feline'."

Jon Arbuckle reached for the television dial. Instantly, Garfield pinned Jon's arm to the chair.

"Do you really want to watch this?" said Jon.

"Do you really want to keep your arm?" replied Garfield.

"We watch too much television," continued Jon. "It's turning our brains to mush."

"In your case, no one will notice."

"Besides, the picture on this old telly is fuzzy. At least let me fix it."

"All right," agreed Garfield. "But remember what happened when you fixed the toaster. It still makes that flushing sound."

Jon grabbed a screwdriver and began tinkering with the back of the telly. "Ah, here's the problem," he said. Suddenly, there was a loud crack. "Yipes!" said Jon. Smoke wafted from the telly. The screen went dead. So did all the lights in Jon's house . . . and in all of the other houses in the road!

"Jon, you're the problem," grumbled Garfield.

It took the electricity company seven hours to restore power to the neighbourhood. But Jon's telly was still blank. Jon called in a television repairman, who frowned, then heaved the telly into the back of his lorry.

"Jon, stop that man!" cried Garfield in a panic.

"It's an old telly," Jon explained to Garfield and Odie. "The repairman said it will take some time to find the right parts. It might not be fixed for a month."

"A month!" cried Garfield. "No telly for a month? No dramas? No game shows? No cat food commercials? What will I do for entertainment?"

"We'll just have to make the best of it," said Jon. "I'm sure there are plenty of other fun things we could do. What did people do before they watched television?"

"They scratched and hoped sabre-tooth tigers wouldn't eat them," said Garfied.

The next day Garfield stomped around the house. "No telly," he mumbled. "Isn't there a law against this? How will I fill up my day? Let's see. What else do I do besides watch the telly? I eat. And I sleep. I sleep! That's the answer!"

Garfield flung himself down on his bed. "I'll sleep for a month," he said. "When I awake, the telly will be fixed." Garfield closed his eyes.

When he awoke, however, it was only 27 hours later. "Guess even a champion napper like me has his limits," said Garfield. "I'll have to try something else to pass the time. Let's see what's playing in the fridge. That should hold my interest for a while."

Garfield ate all the food in the fridge. He ate all the food in the pantry. He ate all the food in the house! Garfield ate enough food to last a lifetime. But Garfield ate it all in a lunchtime. "Unfortunately, I'm a speed-eater," he said.

Perhaps Jon was doing something interesting. Garfield padded into the bedroom to find out.

"Hey, Garfield," said Jon. "Want to help me rearrange my sock drawer? It's really fun. See? I'm grouping the pairs by colour. Now, what do you think I should do with the patterned ones?"

"Stuff them up your nose."

"When I'm finished here, I'm going to fluff the bristles on my toothbrush."

"Jon, you're reaching new depths of dullness," said Garfield, turning and walking quickly out of the room.

Garfield spotted Odie in the living room. "Well," said Garfield, with a shrug, "when all else fails, abuse the dog." Garfield sneaked up behind Odie. He snatched Odie's tongue and began winding it around the confused dog. "Hey, Odie! Want to go for a spin?" asked Garfield. He gave Odie's tongue a yank, and the dog twirled swiftly around the room, bouncing off the furniture like a pinball! Before the dizzy dog could recover, Garfield did it again. And again. And again! Odie spun and spun. "You know," said Garfield, "this looks like fun at first, but the enjoyment wears off after the first fifty times. Sorry, old pal," he said to Odie, "you'll have to amuse yourself for a while."

Garfield paced the rug. "A telly, a telly. My kingdom for a telly!" he muttered. "If I don't find something to occupy my mind, I'm going to lose it! If only I could be like Jon and spend happy hours watching my toenails grow. But, no! My brain needs stimulation. I need a telly! Any telly! Even a picture of a telly will do!"

That gave Garfield an idea. He ran to Jon's library and went straight to the encyclopedia. Pulling out the volume marked "T", Garfield flipped through the pages until he came to a picture of a television. "It's not much, but I feel a little bit better," said Garfield, with a sigh.

On the page was a detailed diagram of the inside of a television. "This looks pretty complicated," observed Garfield. "No wonder Jon couldn't figure it out. I mean, the man can barely work a zip." Garfield examined the picture more closely. "Hmmm. Very interesting," he said. He flipped a few more pages. There was a drawing of William Tell, the Swiss hero, aiming his crossbow at an apple on his son's head. "This looks pretty exciting," thought Garfield. Further on in the book he looked at an article on tennis. Later, he paused to learn about the Thames, Tibet, and tigers!

"Garfield! Time for dinner!" called Jon.

Garfield looked up from his book. "Already?" he said. "Where did the day go?"

Garfield began to spend a lot of time in Jon's library. There was so much interesting information! The cat books were his favourites. But he also worked his way through an entire cookbook. And when the telly returned, Garfield barely noticed.

"Come on, Garfield," said Jon. "It's time to watch our programmes."

Garfield shook his head. "Jon, you watch too much television," he said. 'I may join you later. But right now, my brain has better things to do!"

GARFIELD'S MONDAY QUIZ

Garfield knows all about Mondays! If he's got to get up before mid-day; if Jon's going to put him on a diet; if a custard pie's going to hit him in the face or he's going to get stuck in the roller-blind – it's bound to happen on a Monday!

But how much do YOU know about Garfield's un-favourite day of the week?

Here are 10 quiz questions to test your 'Monday-ology':

1 'I Don't Like Mondays' was a big hit record by the pop group, The Boomtown Rats. Who was their famous lead singer?

2 Up until quite recently, what did housewives always do on a Monday?

3 Monday is the first day of the week. True or false?

4 Monday is named after the Moon. True or false?

5 According to an ancient rhyme, Sunday's Child was full of Grace. What was Monday's Child?

6 According to another old poem, who was born on a Monday, Christened on a Tuesday, married on a Wednesday and so on?

 7 One of BBC television's longest-running series is always shown on a Monday. What is it called?

 9 The first ever Garfield newspaper strip was published on a Monday. True or false?

 8 One of ITV's longest-running shows is also shown on a Monday (and other days of the week). What is it called?

 10 In the United Kingdom, Bank Holidays always occur on a Monday. True or false?

Answers

1. Bob Geldof
2. Their washing
3. False. Sunday is officially the first day of the week
4. True
5. Fair of face
6. Solomon Grundy
7. Panorama
8. Coronation Street
9. True. On June 19th, 1978
10. False. Certain Bank Holidays such as New Year's Day occur on a different day each year.

Garfield's famed as a big, fat cat,

(He's really rather proud of that!)

But there are others, bigger than he,

Who don't eat lasagne for their tea,

Famed for their beauty, power and grace,

Masters of the feline race . . .

THE BIG CATS

THE LION

THE LION, most common of the big cats, lives on the plains of Africa. It preys upon the large herds of grass-eating animals such as wildebeest, deer and zebra. Lions are are known to hunt by day, but more often they hunt at night when it is cooler. They catch their prey in a variety of ways, sometimes stalking their victim until it is exhausted or rushing in with a

Picturepoint – London

powerful burst of speed and bowling it over. They never kill more than they need, and what is left over often provides a meal for other animals such as hyenas. Once full, lions retire to the shade and doze until hunger drives them to hunt again.

Picturepoint – London

THE TIGER

THE TIGER is Asia's big cat. This magnificent animal, the largest member of the cat family, is found in varying forms in places as far apart as Siberia and Malaysia. It is a solitary animal that likes to inhabit forests, grassy areas and swamps. Unlike most other cats, the tiger likes water and can swim very well. It is a fierce hunter and has been known to attack elephants and buffalo, although it mainly feeds on deer, wild pigs and fowl. Sometimes, an old or injured tiger finds human beings an easy prey and so becomes a man-eater!

THE LEOPARD

THE LEOPARD is found in both Africa and Asia.
The African Leopard is a very secretive animal, living on the plains near the edge of the forests. It likes to catch its prey by leaping down from an overhanging branch or bursting out of undergrowth to take its victim by surprise.

Picturepoint – London

The Asian Leopard is equally at home in forests, swamps, grassy plains or semi-deserts. It also likes to ambush its prey, often hanging its kill on a tree to keep it away from scavengers. Black Asian leopards are known as PANTHERS. Another variant, the SNOW LEOPARD or OUNCE, lives on the slopes of the Himalaya Mountains. These animals are now very rare.

Picturepoint – London

THE LYNX

THE LYNX is a short-tailed big cat that lives in the forests of Europe, Asia and Canada. It has long legs, large paws and distinctive tufts of hair on its ears. It is a silent, nocturnal animal that can climb and swim very well. It eats birds, rabbits and small deer.

Picturepoint – London

THE OCELOT

THE OCELOT is found in the southern parts of the USA (Texas) and in South America. It is also a forest-dweller that hunts at night for birds and small mammals. It is famous for its very beautiful fur.

Picturepoint – London

THE COUGAR

THE COUGAR is the big cat of North America. It inhabits high ground such as The Rocky Mountains and catches the goats, sheep and deer that graze on the mountain slopes. Sometimes known as the Mountain Lion, the cougar is a powerful and athletic hunter that is quite capable of dragging a carcase three times its own weight.

Picturepoint – London

THE CHEETAH

THE CHEETAH is the fastest animal in the world (on land). It only hunts during the day and can catch even the fastest antelope by sheer speed. However, it often stalks its prey for a long time before making a final rush and, if the intended victim escapes, the cheetah usually gives up. It cannot run at top speed for more than about two hundred metres without becoming exhausted. Occasionally, cheetahs have been trained to hunt for Man, but because they tire so quickly, they have to be carried until the prey is in sight!

SPOT THE DIFFERENCE

There are 10 differences between these two pictures of Garfield playing with his toys. Some are easy to spot; others are much more difficult. Can you find them all? The answers are printed at the bottom of the page.

'GAT~TOTHED WAS SHE'

The feature for which Arlene is most famous is that huge gap in her front teeth. If you remember, Garfield is always teasing her about it and Arlene usually gets very miffed!

In fact, Arlene is not alone in possessing widely-spaced front teeth. It appears to be a well-known dental phenomenon called DIASTEMA which is common throughout the population. It has also been recognised and commented upon for centuries. The first person whose front teeth get a special mention is a very unusual lady indeed . . .

'GAT-TOTHED WAS SHE, SOOTHLY FOR TO SEYE.
UP-ON AN AMBLERE ESILY SHE SAT,
Y-WIMPLED WEL, AND ON HIR HEED A HAT
AS BROOD AS IS A BOKELER OR A TARGE;'

(SHE HAD A GAP IN HER TEETH, TRUTH TO TELL.
SHE SAT CONFIDENTLY ON HER HORSE,
WEARING A WIMPLE AND A HAT
THAT WAS AS BIG AS A SHIELD OR TARGET;)

The Wife of Bath

Geoffrey Chaucer

So wrote the poet, Geoffrey Chaucer (1340-1400), in his best-known work, the Canterbury Tales. In this long series of poems written in early English, some pilgrims travelling from London to the shrine of St Thomas à Becket at Canterbury tell each other stories to pass the time on their journey.

One of these pilgrims is THE WIFE OF BATH and the lines opposite are part of Chaucer's description of her. She is a stout, well-dressed lady who has travelled the world (quite an achievement in those days) and been married five times!

Why does Chaucer mention that The Wife Of Bath has a gap in her front teeth? Well, it seems that people in the Middle Ages believed that anyone with this appearance had:

A LOVING DISPOSITION!

Is this true of Arlene?
It would seem so!
After all, Arlene needs to have a loving disposition – and MORE – to put up with being Garfield's girlfriend!

29

GARFIELD ALL AT SEA

Lone yachtsman Garfield approaches harbour at the end of a long voyage. On the quayside, Arlene waits patiently for her hero to return. But a number of dangers face the intrepid sailor before he can be reunited with his girlfriend. Can YOU help Garfield to steer a path through these perilous waters?

GIVE SOMEONE
A CUDDLE
FOR
CHRISTMAS!

A PICTURE TO COLOUR

Garfield's Top Twenty

Since Garfield first burst on the scene in June 1978, Jim Davis has drawn a staggering total of nearly 4,500 Garfield comic strips. Every day he adds a new strip to this total and Garfield now appears in over 2,100 different newspapers around the world, delighting an audience of hundreds of millions.

In all this time, we wondered if Jim Davis had any favourite Garfield strips – ones which have given him particular pleasure to think up and draw, or which have stuck in his memory as being particularly funny. So we asked him to select the 20 Garfield daily strips which he likes best and we have printed these classics on the following five pages. They are not numbered 1-20 because they are not in order of merit. (There are too many great Garfield strips to be as selective as that!) Garfield's Top Twenty is just the best of 12 years of Garfield.

36

I THINK YOU'LL ENJOY FLYING, GARFIELD

IT'S A VERY COMFORTABLE AND SMOOTH WAY TO TRAVEL

THEN WHAT ARE THESE LITTLE BAGS FOR? THE EASTER EGG HUNT?

I AM DOWN... DOWN, DOWN, DOWN, DOWN, DOWN

DOWN, DOWN, DOWN, DOOBY DOO DOWN, DOWN

COMMA, COMMA, DOWN DOOBY DOO DOWN, DOWN

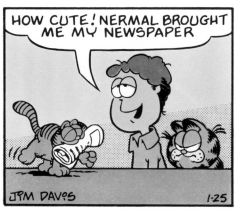

HOW CUTE! NERMAL BROUGHT ME MY NEWSPAPER

AND MY SLIPPERS AND MY PIPE! WHAT MORE COULD A MAN WANT?

HOW ABOUT A WOMAN?

HOW DO YOU WANT YOUR COFFEE, GARFIELD?

MAKE IT SIT UP AND BARK

HOW'S THIS?

JUST RIGHT

40

Other GARFIELD Greats

What's in a name? Quite a lot, it seems! In last year's annual (page 32), it was revealed that Garfield is named after Jim Davis's grandfather, James A. Garfield Davis. But where did Mr. Davis Senior get the name from? What does the name mean? And does the world's best-known cat share his name with any other famous people?

After a great deal of exhaustive research, the answers to these questions can now be revealed. . . .

According to a dictionary of American names, 'GARFIELD' means:

'DWELLER ON THE GRASSY LAND OR PASTURE'

The dictionary states that the name is of English origin, but the actual name 'Garfield' does not appear in any similar dictionaries of English family names. So it would seem that its early use was exclusively American.

I THINK GARFIELD MEANS 'GREAT'!

The name 'Garfield' became famous with the election of James Garfield as 20th President of the United States in November, 1880. President Garfield had only been in office for 4 months when he was attacked and severely wounded by a rival at the railway station in Washington D.C. The unfortunate President never recovered from the attack and was succeeded by Vice President Chester A. Arthur in November 1881.

James Garfield, 1880

Picturepoint – London

To honour President Garfield, several places in America changed their name to Garfield – Garfield City in New Jersey and Garfield Heights in Cleveland, Ohio, being cases in point. In addition, many people adopted the name Garfield as an extra middle name.

Garfield shares his famous name with two modern celebrities, a cricketer and a writer.

SIR GARFIELD SOBERS is one of the greatest cricketers of all time. Born on July 28th, 1936, in Bridgetown, Barbados, Sobers's cricketing talent was evident from a very early age and he began playing test matches for the West Indies when still only 17. During his test career, which lasted from 1953 until 1974, he scored an amazing total of 8032 runs in 160 innings (21 of them not out). This is a world record which nobody has yet surpassed.

Sir Garfield also holds another world record, that of the most runs scored off a single over. On August 31st, 1968, while playing for Nottinghamshire against Glamorgan at Swansea, he scored the maximum 36 runs from a six-ball over by hitting six consecutive sixes,

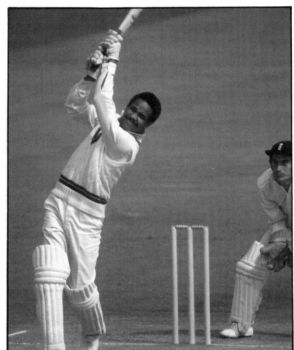

Sir Garfield Sobers

Picturepoint – London

the last huge strike sending the ball right out of the ground where it was retrieved by a small boy from the street. To date, no-one else has managed to emulate this feat and, to record the event, the cricket ball is now on display in Nottingham Museum.

LEON GARFIELD, the writer, is well-known for his books about low-life in 18th Century London. The most famous of them is 'SMITH' which won the Arts Council Award for best book for Older Children 1966-8 and was runner-up for the Carnegie Medal in 1967.

Leon Garfield is one of a number of children's writers who completely changed the style of children's books during the 1960s and 70s. Instead of writing swashbuckling yarns about improbable heroes, his stories feature poor children (usually on the outskirts of society) and are based on accurate research, realism and a genuine feel for the past. Reading a Leon Garfield book is like taking a trip back in time.

MUNCH MUNCH MUNCH

DON'T YOU THINK YOU'VE EATEN ENOUGH WATERMELON, GARFIELD?

WHY, NO

WHY DO YOU ASK?

PTOO!

KICK!

I'M SORRY GARFIELD. I DIDN'T SEE YOU SITTING...

THERE

Z

N

GARFIELD'S REVOLTING M

The mice are revolting! No, that's not the opinion of Jon's latest girlfriend – it's a fact! The mice in Garfield's house are staging a revolution. "Out with the cat!" they cry.

Garfield realises this is all his fault. "If I had not adopted my 'live and let live' approach to the mice," he thinks, "this would not have happened." So Garfield decides to fight back. But it's one against many. Will you help Garfield to put the mice in their place by joining in his game of cat-and-mouse?

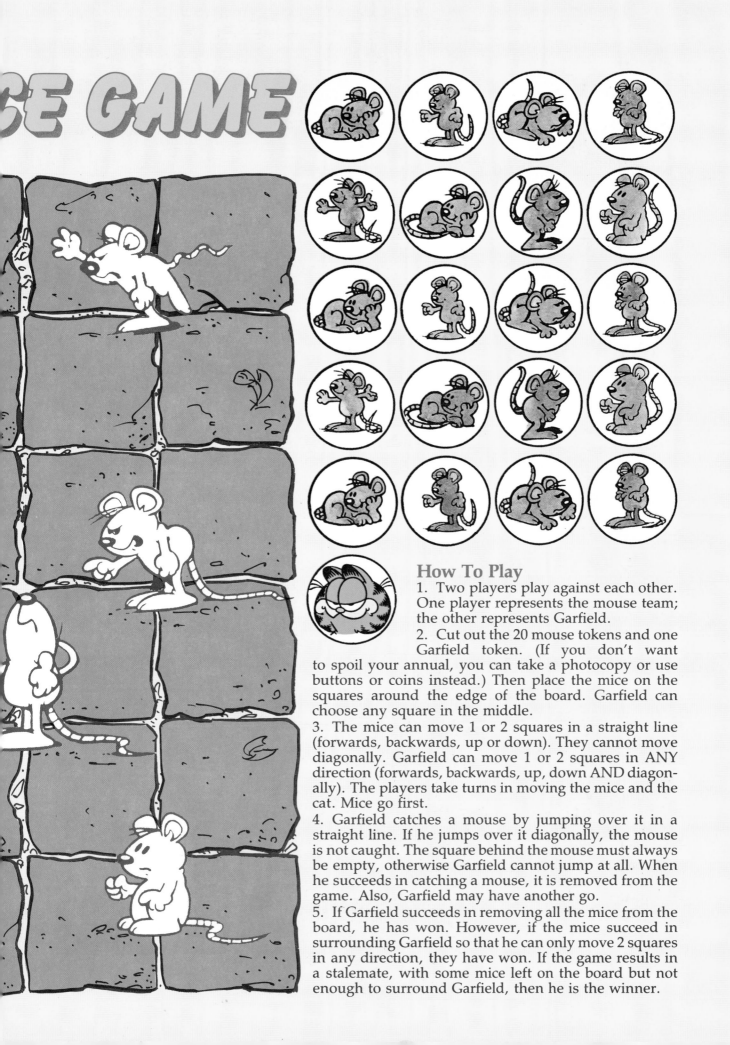

CE GAME

How To Play

1. Two players play against each other. One player represents the mouse team; the other represents Garfield.

2. Cut out the 20 mouse tokens and one Garfield token. (If you don't want to spoil your annual, you can take a photocopy or use buttons or coins instead.) Then place the mice on the squares around the edge of the board. Garfield can choose any square in the middle.

3. The mice can move 1 or 2 squares in a straight line (forwards, backwards, up or down). They cannot move diagonally. Garfield can move 1 or 2 squares in ANY direction (forwards, backwards, up, down AND diagonally). The players take turns in moving the mice and the cat. Mice go first.

4. Garfield catches a mouse by jumping over it in a straight line. If he jumps over it diagonally, the mouse is not caught. The square behind the mouse must always be empty, otherwise Garfield cannot jump at all. When he succeeds in catching a mouse, it is removed from the game. Also, Garfield may have another go.

5. If Garfield succeeds in removing all the mice from the board, he has won. However, if the mice succeed in surrounding Garfield so that he can only move 2 squares in any direction, they have won. If the game results in a stalemate, with some mice left on the board but not enough to surround Garfield, then he is the winner.

NERMAL'S KITTEN QUIZ

A page especially for Garfield's younger readers

Here are 6 questions all about little cats like Nermal, the world's cutest kitten.

How many can you answer?

1. What is the proper name for a group of newly-born kittens?

CLUE: Bits of paper dropped on the ground!

2. In America, they call it 'shedding'. In Britain, we call it 'moulting'. All kittens do it. What does it mean?

(a) Hiding in the garden shed
(b) Losing hair
(c) Scratching the furniture

3. Some kittens are born without tails.
(a) True?
(b) False?

4. Is it wrong to pick up a kitten by the scruff of its neck?

5. In one part of the United Kingdom, you can still find kittens that are completely wild. Which part?

(a) England
(b) Scotland
(c) Wales
(d) Northern Ireland
(e) Eire

CLUE: They live in the mountains.

6. (a) How many lives are cats and kittens supposed to have?

(b) How many do they really have?

A PRESENT FOR JON

While Garfield and Odie were enjoying their breakfast one morning, Jon carefully examined his calendar. "Well, let's see what day this is," said Jon, loudly. "Why, what do you know? It's my birthday!" He glanced at his pets to see if they were paying attention. "My birthday," he continued. "My very own, once a year birthday. Gee, I wonder if my pets know that today is my birthday?"

Garfield scowled. "We know, we know," he said. "Also we know that we don't care."

"Wouldn't it be great if my pets did something special for me today?" Jon continued. "Something to show how much they appreciate all the love and attention I give them, hint, hint?"

"Wouldn't it be great if you stuffed a sock in your mouth, hint, hint?" replied Garfield.

"Well, I'll just be hanging around the house today," said Jon, heading for the living room, "in case certain pets want to shower me with affection."

"I'd rather kiss a pit bull," grumbled Garfield.

When Jon had gone, Garfield looked at Odie. "You know what this means," said Garfield. "Either we do something nice for Jon or he slips into a major depression. He might get too depressed to make dinner. Which would definitely depress me."

"Hmmm," said Odie, frowning.

"So here's the plan. After breakfast I'll pop over to the precinct and pick up a nice present for Jon. In the meantime, you can go in there and do something cute and affectionate. Like slobber on his shoes."

Later that morning Garfield strolled into the shopping precinct. "Wow! Look at all of these shops!" he exclaimed. "I'm sure to find something that's perfect for Jon. I'll just look for a shop that specialises in bad taste."

Garfield entered a men's clothing store. He saw racks of suits, stacks of shirts, and hundreds of ties. But none of them seemed right for Jon. "Jon has his own style," thought Garfield. "It's not exactly 'Saville Row'. It's more like 'Geek Street'."

Garfield approached an assistant at the tie counter. "Excuse me," said Garfield. "Do you have any ties for a man who looks bad in everything? I'd prefer something that requires batteries."

The assistant looked up at Garfield and cringed. "Ugh! Get out of here, cat!" cried the man. "Shoo! Before you shed hair all over the merchandise!"

"Okay, okay, I'm leaving," said Garfield, leaving a trail of cat hair behind.

Garfield's next stop was an electrical shop. "Let's see. Jon already has a televison," said Garfield. "And sometimes I even let him watch what he wants. He has a fridge, though we could always use two. I wonder if they have any automatic cat feeders?"

Then Garfield noticed the stereo systems. "Now there's an idea!" he said. "Jon's stereo hasn't sounded the same since I fed Odie's tongue into the tape deck." Garfield listened to one of the stereos. "This one sounds good," he observed. "It has a turntable, cassette deck, radio, and CD player. But there's still one very important thing to check."

Garfield smashed his fist down on the stereo. The music screeched to a stop. "Too bad," said Garfield. "It's obviously not pet-proof."

"Hey, cat! What are you doing?" yelled an assistant. "Get out of here before you ruin all of our equipment!"

Garfield had to run for the door. "If they don't want you to bash the merchandise, they should put up a sign," said Garfield.

Back out in the precinct, Garfield suddenly stopped and sniffed the air. A deliciously familiar aroma was wafting his way. "Pizza!" said Garfield, licking his lips. "To be precise, deep dish pizza topped with 24 slices of pepperoni and four ounces of sausage, baked by a woman with a tattoo of Elvis on her arm."

Garfield followed his nose to the pizza parlour. And sure enough, there on the counter was the pizza he had described. And behind the counter was a large woman with a tattoo of Elvis on her right forearm.

Garfield hopped up on the counter beside the pizza. The woman stood with her back to him, kneading pizza dough. "No need to see the menu," Garfield said to the woman. "Just bring me one of everything, with more of everything on the side. And for an appetiser, I'll have dessert."

Of course, the woman, being unable to hear Garfield's thoughts, went right on with her pizza making.

"All right. Don't trouble yourself," Garfield said. "I'll just help myself."

Garfield picked up a slice of pizza. Just then, the woman turned around. "Hey!" she shouted. "Get away from there, you fat cat!" She swung a large spatula at Garfield, who had to leap out of the way. Garfield ran for the door. "I'll say one thing for that place," said Garfield. "The service may be slow, but it's rude."

Garfield left the precinct in disgust. "All I wanted was a cheap, tasteless present for Jon," he grumbled. "And what did I get? Abuse! Nothing but abuse! What's the matter with those assistants, anyway? Does Jon get upset if I leave a few thousand cat hairs on his clothes? Does Jon yell at me if I break his expensive stereo? Does Jon try to swat me if I steal his food? Of course he does! But he doesn't try to drive me away," said Garfield, thoughtfully. "And he continues to feed me and take care of me. And he never stays cross for long." Garfield scratched his chin. "Hmmm. I guess Jon must really love me. Either that, or he's a glutton for punishment."

Garfield ran the rest of the way home. Fortunately for Garfield, this was only about ten metres. He burst into the living room and leaped onto Jon's lap.

"Garfield! What's going on?" said Jon.

"Happy Birthday, Jon," said Garfield, giving Jon a big hug.

"Does this mean you appreciate me?" asked Jon.

"I do, Jon," said Garfield. "I really do. And that's why I'm going to say those three little words that truly express my deepest feelings at this moment."

Garfield smiled at Jon. Jon smiled at Garfield.

"Let's have lunch," said Garfield.

58

CHRISTMAS CAN'T BE OVER YET! I CAN'T HAVE UNWRAPPED ALL MY PRESENTS ALREADY!!

I GOTTA UNWRAP SOMETHING ELSE!!

© 1987 United Feature Syndicate, Inc.

MORE! MORE!

12-26

THIS YEAR I PLEDGE TO LOSE WEIGHT AND GET IN SHAPE!

© 1987 United Feature Syndicate, Inc.

NO, NO, BE REALISTIC, GARFIELD. THAT'S A BIT MUCH TO BITE OFF. PERHAPS I SHOULD SET A BIT MORE REALISTIC GOAL.

I PLEDGE TO ESTABLISH CONTACT WITH ALIENS FROM ANOTHER PLANET!

JIM DAVIS 12-29

WELL, IT'S TIME TO TAKE STOCK OF THE YEAR

© 1987 United Feature Syndicate, Inc.

LET'S SEE... I ATE AND SLEPT AND ACCOMPLISHED NOT ONE SINGLE THING OF SOCIALLY REDEEMING VALUE

I'M SO PROUD OF ME

JIM DAVIS 12-30

LET'S SEE. THIS YEAR I'VE EATEN 2,190 SNACKS AND TAKEN 1,822 NAPS

© 1987 United Feature Syndicate, Inc.

OH, NO! ACCORDING TO MY FIGURES I MISSED A NAP IN APRIL AND TWO IN JULY!

UH... GARFIELD?

QUIET, MAN! I HAVE SOME SERIOUS CATCHING UP TO DO!

JIM DAVIS 12-31